Where there
~Burundian pr

A united family eats from the same plate. ~ Baganda proverb

However long the night, the dawn will break. ~ African proverb

Wisdom is wealth. ~ Swahili

Sticks in a bundle are unbreakable. ~ Bondei proverb

Milk and honey have different colors, but they share the same house peacefully. ~ African proverb

Wisdom is like a baobab tree, no one individual can embrace it. ~ Akan proverb

Only a wise person can solve a difficult problem. ~ Akan proverb

The fool speaks, the wise man listens. ~ Ethiopian proverb

Many hands make light work. ~ Tanzania proverb

A flea can trouble a lion more than a lion can trouble a flea.~ Kenyan proverb

There can be no peace without understanding. ~Senegalese proverb

We desire to bequeath two things to our children, the first one is roots, the other one is wings. ~Sudanese proverb

By trying often, the monkey learns to jump from the tree. ~ Buganda proverb

The heart of the wise man lies quiet like limpid water. ~ Cameroon proverb

Be a mountain or lean on one. ~Somali proverb

You do not teach the paths of the forest to an old gorilla. ~Congolese proverb

The food that is in the mouth is not yet in the belly. ~Kikuyu Proverb

An army of sheep led by a lion can defeat an army of lions led by a sheep. ~ Ghanaian proverb

Knowledge without wisdom is like water in the sand. ~ Guinean proverb

Instruction in youth is like engraving in stone.
~Moroccan Proverb

Nobody knows the beginning of a great man.
~Akan proverb

In the moment of crisis, the wise build bridges and the foolish build dams. ~ Nigerian proverb

A united family eats from the same plate. ~ Baganda proverb

The best and shortest road towards knowledge of truth is Nature. ~Egyptian

If your only tool is a hammer, you will see every problem as a nail. ~Gambian proverb

Do not let the goat you might carry on your shoulder play in the mud. ~Mende proverb

A fight between grasshoppers is a joy to the crow. ~ Lesotho proverb

He who is unable to dance says that the yard is stony. ~Masai proverb

When you show the moon to a child, it sees only your finger. ~Zambian proverb

The friends of our friends are our friends.
~ Congolese proverb

A crab does not give birth to a bird. ~Akan proverb

If you pick up one end of the stick you also pick up the other. ~Ethiopian proverb

Do a good deed and throw it into the sea.
~Egyptian proverb

A wise person will always find a way.
~Tanzanian proverb

You think of water when the well is empty.~Ethiopia proverb

It is not necessary to blow out the other person's lantern to let yours shine.~Swahili proverb

Even the lion, the king of the forest, must protect himself from flies. ~Ghanaian proverb

It is when you climb a good tree that we push you up.~Ghanaian proverb

Learning expands great souls. ~ Namibian proverb

A large chair does not make a king. ~
Sudanese proverb

Birds sing not because they have answers but because they have songs. ~African proverb

Children are the reward of life. ~ African proverb

Advice is a stranger, if he's welcome he stays for the night, if not, he leaves the same day. ~Malagasy Proverb

When the roots of a tree begin to decay, it spreads death to the branches. ~Nigerian proverb

He who fears the sun will not become chief.
~Ugandan proverb

When the shepherd comes home in peace, the milk is sweet. ~Ethiopian proverb

The most beautiful fig may contain a worm.
~Zulu Proverb

By the time the fool has learned the game, the players have dispersed. ~Ashanti proverb

Hold a true friend with both hands. ~ African proverb

A bird that flies off the earth and lands on an anthill is still on the ground. ~Igbo proverb

If you want to go quickly, go alone. If you want to go far, go together. ~ African proverb

Made in United States
Troutdale, OR
09/19/2024